ANDREW LANG

ANDREW LANG

Andrew Lang

Roger Lancelyn Green

A WALCK MONOGRAPH
GENERAL EDITOR: KATHLEEN LINES

HENRY Z. WALCK, INCORPORATED
NEW YORK

BY THE SAME AUTHOR

Tellers of Tales
Andrew Lang
A. E. W. Mason
Fifty Years of 'Peter Pan'
Into Other Worlds
The Story of Lewis Carroll
Lewis Carroll (Walck Monograph)
J. M. Barrie (Walck Monograph)
etc.

Library of Congress Catalog Card Number: 62-18333
© The Bodley Head Ltd 1962
First American Edition 1962
Printed in Great Britain

CONTENTS

Dedicated to

B. MEREDITH LANGSTAFF

Of Andrew Lang I tell again;
Dear Meredith, do not disdain
This trifle, though but slim in looks.
As smallest freshets fill the brooks,
As countless rivers seek the main,
So this my work will not be vain
If it finds place—one tiny grain
In your rich harvest of the books
    Of Andrew Lang.

So take this love-child of my brain,
This tribute paid 'twixt bookmen twain
Whose chief delight is in the nooks
Where bargains linger. . . . Ah, but flukes
We need, who every work would gain
    Of Andrew Lang!

A Note about the Author

A house full of books took the place of a more formal education for Roger Lancelyn Green until he went to Oxford, and it was his enthusiasm for the stories of Rider Haggard which first led him, at the age of ten, to Andrew Lang, Haggard's collaborator in *The World's Desire*. This later became his favourite book and inspired him to ask what else Lang had written. His 'literary' godfather, Gordon Bottomley, thereupon introduced him to the poetry and critical essays of Lang, which formed the foundation of his knowledge of English literature. When he went up to Oxford, he discovered that his own college, Merton, had been Lang's college, too, and he chose Lang as the subject of the thesis he presented for his B.Litt.

Roger Lancelyn Green now lives at Poulton-Lancelyn, the manor house where his ancestors have lived for nine hundred years. He has already contributed to this series studies of *Lewis Carroll*, *J. M. Barrie*, and *Mrs Molesworth*.

Acknowledgments

Andrew Lang did not wish a biography or collection of his letters to appear, and his widow obeyed his behest with heart-rending thoroughness: 'My wrists ached for weeks after tearing up Andrew's papers,' she told one of her nieces. The same scrupulous care was taken by Lang's favourite cousin Florence Sellar (Mrs MacCunn) and the most notable of his child-friends, Dorothea Thorpe (Lady Charnwood).

When I came to collect the material for *Andrew Lang: A Critical Biography* (1946) the material open to me was almost entirely that contained in his own published works, and in the biographies and reminiscences of his contemporaries. The only personal contact was that I had spent one evening with Mrs MacCunn (aged eighty and stone deaf) just before going to Merton as an undergraduate, and had several letters from her during the next two years. She used to say that the wheel had come full circle: here she was addressing letters to Merton in a big, shaky hand (owing to age)—the last letters she had written to the same address had also been in a big shaky hand (owing to extreme youth): but the superscription was then to Andrew Lang. She died before I thought of writing about Lang, but her last surviving sister Mrs M. V. Dent read my book and wrote (almost from her death-bed) in commendation of it: 'I think it is quite extraordinary that you—who never knew him—

should have grasped and understood his personality so exactly.'

The book also led to a much valued friendship with Lady Fayrer, daughter of Andrew Lang's favourite brother John, and the present monograph is enriched by many quotations from the only batch of family letters which have survived. There is, naturally, a considerable over-lap with my previous book, but the chance of writing about Lang again has allowed me to correct several errors and include a certain amount of material which I have discovered since: for my researches into the life and works of my favourite author have never ceased and are never likely to do so.

Others who have helped me in my life-long quest after Andrew Lang whom I should like to mention here are Mrs Lang's niece Miss F. M. Alleyne; Mr Mark Longman, and Mr Cyprian Blagden; Miss Lilias Rider Haggard; Mr Alban Dobson; Miss Averil Stewart; Miss Marion Grieve; Mr G. H. Bushnell of St Andrews University Library which contains the best public collection of Lang's works this side of the Atlantic (it is rivalled by the Falconer Collection in Indiana State Library); and my friend Mr B. Meredith Langstaff, who owns the best Lang collection in private hands (I rank my own as second!) and, once again, Professor D. Nichol Smith of Merton College to whom the original biography owed so much.

Finally, among those who are no longer living to receive my thanks, I should like to mention, besides Mrs MacCunn and Mrs Dent, Miss T. B. Alleyne, A. E. W. Mason, Gilbert Murray, Sir W. A. Craigie, Sir D'Arcy Wentworth Thompson, H. W. Garrod, and Mrs Harrison (Nellie Roberts).

R.L.G.

1. One Foot in Fairyland

'And going where this pathway goes
You too, at last may find—who knows?
The garden of the Singing Rose.'

Andrew Lang, 'he who best knew Fairyland', was
born in the long low house of 'Viewfield' at Selkirk
in the Scottish Border country on March 31, 1844,
the eldest child of John Lang the Sheriff-Clerk,
whose father, Andrew, had held the same office
and been a trusted friend of Sir Walter Scott.

From the beginning he, and the five brothers
and a sister who followed him, dwelt in a land of
romance and legend, though only Andrew, who
seems to have been delicate and retiring from an
early age, was influenced by it so strongly that it
had an important effect on all his subsequent
career.

'It was worth while to be a boy then in the south
of Scotland', he wrote, 'and to fish the waters
haunted by old legends, musical with old songs. . . .
Memory brings vividly back the golden summer
evenings by Tweedside, when the trout began to
plash in the stillness—brings back the long, loung-
ing solitary days beneath the woods of Ashiesteil—
days so lonely that they sometimes, in the end,
begat a superstitious eeriness. One seemed forsaken
in an enchanted world; one might see the two
white fairy deer flit by, bringing to us, as to Thomas
the Rhymer, the tidings that we must back to
Fairyland.'

'A boy of five is more at home in Fairyland than

in his own country,' said Lang when telling of his earliest adventures among books: but the Border country all about him was as much on the edge of Fairyland when he lived there as a boy as it was in the days of Flodden Field of which he was to write in *The Gold of Fairnilee*. If he never met anyone who had seen a fairy, his father and the older people of Selkirk remembered those who had. He and a group of small boys would gather on a Saturday evening to hear tales told by an old shepherd and swap such as they themselves had gathered: old Nancy, Lang's own nurse at Viewfield, had a fund of local stories and traditions at her command.

From her Andrew, and his brothers, heard not only fairytales but legends 'about hidden treasures and buried gold'—notably that said to be concealed near the old ruined house of Fairnilee above the Tweed where the Fairy Queen in the Ballad trysted with Thomas the Rhymer. Fairnilee was a favourite haunt of Andrew and his brothers, with such other young friends as Alexander Roberts who was later to build the modern house (now the seat of Lord Craigmyle) which has the ruin in its garden.

'In very truth it is itself a fairyland,' wrote Andrew's youngest brother John of Fairnilee in 1913, 'and, standing here, to the mind comes, irresistibly, thought of the hidden Gold of Fairnilee that in boyhood one sought for so diligently.'

Apart from his reading, and his early interest in fishing and cricket, of which he was always ready to write, little can be gleaned concerning Andrew Lang's childhood, for he left no reminiscences and discouraged others from doing so; he kept no letters and his widow saw to it that no papers survived.

Of Andrew's home at Selkirk the only glimpse comes from a child, the sister of Alexander Roberts, who used frequently to visit Viewfield to play with his sister. Nearly ninety years later she could still remember it as 'a beautiful house with a lovely nursery', and the general feeling of happiness and well-being among the children there. Andrew himself she remembered only as 'a boy buried in a book, and quite oblivious to his surroundings, and certainly with no use for little girls.' He was, however, sociable enough with other boys, joining them not only in collecting fairy lore, but in the favourite Border sports of cricket and fishing.

'The first time I ever saw ball and bat must have been about 1850,' he wrote. 'The gardener's boy and his friends were playing with home-made bats, made out of firwood with the bark on, and with a gutta-percha ball. The game instantly fascinated me.' This was the one game in which Lang showed real skill: as he grew up he joined the local team and played in many exciting matches against the other Border towns. When, as an undergraduate, he put in a term at Loretto (scene, he says, of 'the most exciting match, I think, in which I ever took part'), his brother John, then a boy at the school, described him as 'a bowler of more than the usual type, of whom we spoke with bated breath as one able to pitch on a sixpence.'

Lang's skill soon began to fail him, owing to ill-health and defective eyesight—for which reasons he never became a good golfer though always keen on the game. But his favourite sport, which he practised until the end of his life, was angling: 'The majority of dwellers on the Border are born to be fishers,' he wrote. 'Like the rest of us in that country, I was born an angler, though under an evil star, for, indeed, my labours have not been blessed, and are devoted to fishing rather than to the catching of fish. . . . My first recollection of the sport must date from about the age of four—the sunlight on a shining bend of a highland stream, and my father, standing in the shallow water, showing me a huge yellow fish.' Next 'I see myself, with a crowd of other little children, sent to fish with crooked pins, for minnows' to be used as bait. Instead, they angled for a larger fish, but 'the parr disdained our baits, and for months I dreamed of what it would have been to capture him, and often thought of him in church. In a moment of profane confidence my younger brother once asked me: "What do *you* do in sermon time? I," said he in a whisper—"mind you don't tell—*I* tell stories to myself about catching trout." To which I added a similar confession, for even so I drove the sermon by.'

When he was a little older stories of fishing gave place to more literary imaginings: 'I remember,' he recalled, 'constructing a romance that the Elders had concealed a treasure behind a panel in the wall which closed my school-master's pew.' The religious doubts and fears which troubled Stevenson so much as a boy seem to have passed Lang by: 'Beyond a strong opinion that I should be a "goat" at the Last Day, I can remember no religious speculations of my own,' he wrote. 'The idea of the Deity made little impression; the Shorter Catechism, which had to be learnt by heart, seemed meaningless, and did not even excite curiosity. . . . I do remember thinking that the Angels who made love to the daughters of men, were the gods—Apollo and Zeus and Hermes—under another name. One's infant reason was mythological, not theological in bias.'

From a very early age the literary bias was a powerful one in Lang's life. He first found his way to the Fairyland which books could reveal to him at the age of four when he learnt to read by memorizing nursery rhymes and then picking them out in print, and had *Robinson Crusoe* read to him. Soon he was obtaining and reading for himself 'chap-books about Robert Bruce, William Wallace and Rob Roy. At that time these little tracts could be bought for a penny apiece. I can still see Bruce in full armour, and Wallace in a kilt, discoursing across a burn.' But he was more readily at home in the Fairy world, and *The White Cat* and *The Yellow Dwarf*, also in chap-books, were 'my first memories of romance. One story of a White Serpent, with a wood-cut of that mysterious reptile, I neglected to secure, probably for want of a penny, and I have regretted it ever since.'

Next came *The Arabian Nights* and Shakespeare to open new worlds of enchantment for him, and he recalled from the age of six 'a picture, more vivid than most, of a small boy reading the *Midsummer Night's Dream* by firelight in a room where candles were lit, and someone touched the piano, and a young man and a girl were playing chess. . . . The fairies seemed to come out of Shakespeare's dream into the music and the firelight.'

The following year 'there was usually a little volume of Scott in one's pocket, in company with the miscellaneous collection of a boy's treasures. . . . Scott peopled for us the rivers and burnsides with his reivers; the Fairy Queen came out of Eildon Hill and haunted Carterhaugh. . . . Scott is not an author like another, but our earliest friend in letters'—certainly for Lang living four miles from Abbotsford, and with many people round about who could still remember 'good Sir Walter'.

To begin with, Lang read only Scott's poems, and in fact the first historical romance which made any impression on him was Mrs J. B. Webb's *Naomi; or the Siege of Jerusalem* (1841) encountered when he was six: 'Who indeed could forget the battering-rams, and the man who cried on the battlements: "Woe, woe to myself and to Jerusalem!" ' The impression was so strong that Lang carried it over into make-believe, and remembered, 'as a Roman engineer, taking part in the siege of Jerusalem, with a battering-ram which, to the eyes of adults, bore the aspect of a long hard round cushion.'

Then came 'books about Red Men', led by James Fenimore Cooper and Mayne Reid, and at once Lang set to work to 'make arrows with stone heads. I bought a tomahawk and, as we had lots of spears and boomerangs from Australia, the poultry used to have rather a rough time of it. I never could do very much with a boomerang, but I could throw a spear to a hair's breadth, as many a chicken had occasion to discover.'

This was while Lang was still living at home and beginning his education as a day-boy at Selkirk Grammar School. At the age of ten he was sent to Edinburgh Academy, living for his first two years 'a rather lonely small boy in the house of an aged relation.' We catch a glimpse of him at this time in a letter written to Andrew's father by George Dundas (afterwards Lord Manor), in 1854 or 1855, from Charlotte Square, Edinburgh: 'I had the pleasure, two or three Saturdays ago, of seeing your son, Master Andrew, here, and was exceedingly amused and entertained by him. He is a clever and very curious little fellow, with more general information than I ever remember to have met in one of his age. . . .'

Although he could quote Gibbon, to the amazement of Mr Dundas, Lang confessed that he wasted most of his time (from the academic point of view) living 'like a young hermit' in a world of books: reading Scott, Dickens, Lever, Dumas, and, when novels were forbidden for a season, turning to Ariosto, Byron, Pope and then Longfellow—his favourite (after Scott) until 'I tried Tennyson, and instantly a new light of poetry dawned, a new music was audible, a new god came into my medley of a Pantheon, a god never to be dethroned.'

After two years with the 'aged relation', Lang was moved into the 'very different and very disagreeable world' of a master's house. In the master himself, D'Arcy Wentworth Thompson, Lang knew himself to be fortunate: 'One can never say how much one owes to a schoolmaster who was a friend of literature, who kept a house full of books, and was himself a graceful scholar and an author;' and long after he wrote to Thompson's son of his father's 'kindness, and, as I think now, sagacity to a morbid, useless little boy.'

Though he was perhaps spared many of the Public School rigours of the *Tom Brown* period, Lang was subjected to some at least of the bullying and thoughtless cruelty which even the best schoolmasters seemed unable to prevent. 'As a humble student of savage life, I have found it necessary to make researches into the manners and customs of boys,' he wrote in 1883: 'If you meet them in the holidays, you find them affable and full of kindness and good qualities. . . . But boys at school and among themselves, left to the wild justice and traditional laws which many generations of boys have evolved, are entirely different beings.' Several of the examples of bullying seem to be drawn from Lang's own experiences at Edinburgh; for example: 'Tall stools were piled up in a pyramid, and the victim was seated on top, near the roof of the room. The other savages brought him down from this bad eminence by hurling other stools at those which supported him.'

On the academic side Lang made a bad start. Unexpectedly, at first he detested the Classical subjects, ploughing wearily through Caesar, Virgil and Horace, and considering Greek as represented by Xenophon and Euripides 'a mere plague and torment'. 'I hated Greek,' he wrote, 'with a deadly and sickening hatred; I hated it like a bully and a thief of time. . . .' But when he began to read Homer, under the inspired guidance of James Stephens Hodson, Rector of Edinburgh Academy, 'from the very first words, in which the Muse is asked to sing the wrath of Achilles, Peleus' son, my mind was altered, and I was the devoted friend of Greek. Here was something worth reading about; here one knew where one was; here was the music of words, here were poetry, pleasure and life. . . .' 'The very sound of the hexameter, that long, inimitable roll of the most various music, was enough to win the heart, even if the words were not understood. But the words proved unexpectedly easy to understand, full as they are of all nobility, all tenderness, all courage, courtesy and romance. The *Morte d'Arthur* itself, which about this time fell into our hands, was not so dear as the *Odyssey*.'

This Homeric awakening canalised Lang's interests and his intellectual energy in the direction of an academic career, the first step towards which was his entry into the University of St Andrews in November 1861, when he went into residence at St Leonard's Hall (now the school), and came under the spell of

> 'The drifting surf, the wintry year,
> The college of the scarlet gown——
> St Andrews by the northern sea,
> That is a haunted town to me!'

'That spring we sought the gardens through
For flowers which ne'er in gardens grew!'

With St Andrews, wrote Lang, 'it was a case of
love at first sight, as soon as I found myself under
the grey sky, and beheld the white flame of the
breakers chasing over the brown wet barrier of the
pier'; and he described his two winters and one
summer there as an undergraduate as 'the happiest
time of my life, ever dear and sacred in memory'.
He was obviously in congenial company, and made
at least one close friend, Henry Brown.

'We settled down to work a little and play a great
deal,' wrote Lang with his usual modesty. The most
important part of the 'play' consisted in writing,
and it is from the St Andrews days that Lang's
first surviving literary efforts date. He certainly had
begun to write while still at school, though nothing
remains from that time: 'It was not in nature that
one should not begin to rhyme for one's self. But
those exercises were seldom even written down;
they lived a little while in a memory which has
lost them long ago.'

At least one friend from Edinburgh, Allan
Menzies, went up to St Andrews with Lang, and
these two soon began *The St Leonard's Magazine*.
'I think Lang wrote most of every number of the
magazine himself,' Menzies remembered in 1912,
'and often illustrated his articles in an arresting
way. When Friday night arrived, and no contributions had come in, we feared we should have no

magazine that week. But it was there, nevertheless, for us in the morning.'

It was, of course, a very amateur affair, this
weekly manuscript compilation: 'I was the editor,'
wrote Lang, 'and usually wrote two-thirds or more
of the *Magazine* on Friday night by the glimmer of
stolen candle-ends'. A selection from the first two
volumes was prepared and printed in February
1863—which is all that now survives—and Lang
described the whole as 'perfectly amazing trash'.
He adds, however, that some of the verse translations from Greek and Latin were just worth
preserving, and in fact two of his own versions
from Catullus may be found in his *Poetical Works*,
which represent his very earliest work.

During 1863 the University produced a properly
printed monthly magazine, and to this Lang
contributed two poems and three essays, none of
which did he consider worth preserving. Two of the
essays, on 'Scottish Nursery Tales' and 'Spiritual-
ism, Medieval and Modern', show that Lang was
already interesting himself in those branches of
folklore which he was to make peculiarly his own.
Apart from the necessary Classical books, what he
took out from the University Library included the
works of most of the medieval 'Magicians' from
Petrus de Abano to Cornelius Agrippa. His interest
in the occult grew from reading Lord Lytton's *A
Strange Story* (1862), one of the most popular
books of the day—'which I continue to think a
most satisfactory romance,' he wrote in 1891—and
he is said to have tried, unsuccessfully, to raise the
Devil in the old tower of St Rule's. His interest in

psychical research continued throughout his life, but only as a branch of his anthropological studies —an antichapel of knowledge in which he was an earnest enquirer but never more than an agnostic.

Lang's proper studies at St Andrews did not suffer by his excursions into the byways of literature and occultism. Indeed his work was of such a high level that it was decided to enter him for the Snell Exhibition to Balliol College. This, the most coveted of Classical scholarships to Oxford, was open to Scotsmen only, but required that part of their education should have taken place at Glasgow University.

To qualify for this, Lang went into what he described as 'undesirable exile' in 1863, keeping up a nostalgic connection with St Andrews by contributing to each number of *The St Leonard's Magazine* from November 1863 until late the following spring, when, being about to sit for his exam, he wrote 'A Prospective Farewell'.

> 'Smell, Glesky: to the gibbous Moon
>   Thy smoke and fog deliver,
> I'll cut your stenches very soon
>   For ever and for ever.'

April saw him elected triumphantly to a Snell Exhibition, after which as 'I had nothing to do, and was nearly dead after a winter at Glasgow University, the Head [H. H. Almond] very kindly allowed me to come to Loretto for the summer term to read Greek with Mr Beilby, fresh from Cambridge.'

How Lang spent the Michaelmas Term 1864 is

uncertain, for he did not matriculate at Oxford until January 1865, but he may have come to Oxford earlier for some private tuition, since he speaks of 'how fair Oxford seemed after the black quadrangle and heavy air of Glasgow' and that 'in one of October's crystal days with the elms not yet stripped of their gold, and with the crimson pall of red leaves swathing the tower of Magdalen, Oxford looks almost as beautiful as in the pomp of spring'.

At Balliol, with Jowett as his tutor, he continued on his brilliant, if somewhat untidy, academic way, taking a First in Classical Moderations in 1866 and in 'Greats' in 1868. There was little time for literary pursuits, though his first poem to reach the London press appeared anonymously in *Once A Week* on January 28, 1868, 'The Siren's Music Heard Again'—very much in the style of Swinburne; an attempt at the Newdigate Prize Poem (also in Swinburnian vein) was unsuccessful, and three gay parodies in *The Oxford Undergraduate's Journal* apparently constitute his only contributions to Oxford journalism before he took his degree.

But he was already famed at Balliol for his essays, and a contemporary, Lord Kilbracken, wrote that Lang 'was brilliant in conversation, took a great interest in games (though he played them badly), and as a writer, was already nearly, if not quite, as admirable as he was in later life, which is saying a good deal. I shall never forget listening to an essay of his on Rabelais, which he read to an audience of two or three at the meeting of a small Essay Club to which he and I as undergraduates belonged: it filled me with amazement, and from that moment I always anticipated for him real greatness as a writer.' [The essay on Rabelais formed the basis of Lang's first prose publication in the professional press, in *Frazer's Magazine* for March 1870.] 'He was, moreover, in the true sense of the word, a poet.'

Apart from such recollections as these, there is even less preserved about Lang at Balliol than at St Andrews. If he made any close friends, there is no record of them, and certainly no one came to take the place of Henry Brown, the dearest of all, who died in 1863. Several of Lang's best poems were inspired by the memory of this lost friend, and it was on his account that he wrote in his most famous poem 'Almae Matres: St Andrews 1862; Oxford, 1865':

'And therefore art though yet more dear,
    O little city grey and sere,
Though shrunken from thine ancient pride
    And lonely by the lonely sea,
Than those fair halls on Isis side
    Where youth an hour came back to me!'

Nevertheless he made many friends at Oxford in the more casual sense, including one who was to influence his future career, Frederick William Longman, his exact contemporary at Balliol, with whose family publishing firm his whole literary life came to be bound up. But literature was still far from Lang's thoughts when he secured his First in Literae Humaniores in 1868, for under Jowett's tutoring it became apparent that, like his mother's brother William Young Sellar (also a past pupil of the Master's), he was to be singled out for an academic career centring in the study of Greek, and he settled down to prepare for a Fellowship examination that December.

First, however, he took a much needed holiday at Selkirk, and on his way back to Oxford in October wrote a pleasantly light-hearted letter to a little girl, his young cousin Adele Sellar, beginning that he is writing only 'because I had no novels or books, and Latin and Greek History and Philosophy, Logic and Metaphysics, Politics and other extras, give me a headache—so you can't expect me to have anything to say', and ending with a delightful account of how to understand Hegel: 'You begin by thinking of *nothing* for a long time, till you're quite sure you grasp the situation, and then you think of *something*, only it must not be anything in particular, and gradually you see that something and nothing are both the same, and there you are!'

However Lang's studies in Philosophy certainly helped him to 'something' by the end of the year, when he won the Open Fellowship to Merton College. He entered into residence the following term, with few duties, but much time for study— which he divided at first between the Classics and medieval French. Many of his admirable verse translations which formed a large part of his first book, *Ballads and Lyrics of Old France*, published at the end of 1871, must have been written during his first and happiest year at Merton, and he seemed to have found his métier with an assured and successful academic career before him.

But the happiness was dimmed in September 1869 when both his parents died within two days of one another—a blow which Lang felt very keenly, in particular the loss of his mother, of whom he wrote the following year:

> 'Twilight, and Tweed, and Eildon Hill,
>   Fair and thrice fair you be;
> You tell me that the voice is still
>   That should have welcomed me.'

Not long after this there was, apparently, an unhappy love affair, which left its mark on Lang's supersensitive nature and seems to have upset him profoundly at the time—though afterwards, in a moment of cynicism, he could write 'No Ideal can survive a daily companionship, and fortunate is the poet who did not marry his first love!'

But the longing for an unfulfilled dream which was always somewhere in the background of Lang's more deeply felt writings, seems to be the key to his character as a poet and romantic. 'He appeared to me,' wrote Desmond MacCarthy, 'as one whose deeper love, out of which he had so seldom written, was for the lips that never could be kissed; as a poet who, all his life, had been homesick for he knew not what.'

Perhaps Lang thought he had found the World's Desire when he walked under the Merton lime trees in the summer of 1871 with—who ever it may have been—and wrote the poem which he did not collect:

'The chestnut tapers burned and fell,
That roses might have tales to tell
  Of sweet words said, or guessed unsaid:
Acacia blossoms dropped like snow,
Flake upon fragrant flake to strew
  A carpet for the lightest tread. . . .'

Nearly twenty years later, staying once more in his old rooms at Merton, he wrote:

'In vain we sought the Singing Rose
  Whereof old legends tell.
Alas! we found it not 'mid those
Within the gray old College close,
  That budded, flowered, and fell——
We found the herb called "Wandering",
And meet no more, no more in Spring.'

Whether or not it had any connection with whatever there was of heartbreak in the years immediately following his parents' death in September 1869, Lang's health broke down alarmingly in the autumn of 1872, and he fled to Mentone on the Riviera suffering from acute lung trouble that seemed at first likely to prove fatal. He returned again for the following winter, on which occasion (January 31, 1874) he first met Robert Louis Stevenson, also 'ordered south' on account of his health. After an initial antipathy on both sides, they became good friends, and Stevenson was visiting Lang at Merton in October of the same year, though it was not until Lang was living in London that they saw much of one another.

For by the beginning of 1874 Lang had decided to leave Oxford when his Fellowship terminated, and was already accepting regular reviewing for *The Academy* in anticipation of his coming dependence on journalism.

Although he wrote in 1891 'unfortunately, life at Oxford is not all beauty and pleasure. Things go wrong somehow. Life drops her happy mask,' Lang's last year at Merton was a happy one. We catch a charming glimpse of him in the recollections of a contemporary Fellow, W. L. Courtney: 'I remember him sitting on a garden seat and translating the *Odyssey*—interrupting, too, his work because a certain Miss Alleyne was coming to see him. On those sunny occasions—it seemed to be always sunshine in the Merton gardens—Homer and the notebooks and the manuscripts were thrown incontinently into my lap till, perhaps, S. H. Butcher or some other friend came to the rescue of Homer and recalled the wandering lover to his task.'

Leonora Blanche Alleyne (1851-1933) was the youngest child of Charles Thomas Alleyne of Clifton, Bristol, and two of her brothers were at Merton, the younger only joining the college in 1873. There is no record of how Lang first met her: there was some family connection with Clifton —indeed he had spent a year of his childhood there, in about 1850—but he may not have met 'Nora' before 1874, in that gay summer season when Oxford makes festival,

'When wickets are bowled and defended,
When Isis is glad with the Eights. . . .

28

When bouquets are purchased of Bates,
When the bells in their melody chime—
Ah, these are the hours that one rates—
Sweet hours and the fleetest of time!'

However it was, this vivid young lady with 'her exuberance of spirit and unquenchable thirst for knowledge and adventure' came into Lang's life at the perfect moment, and brought him the quiet happiness (as well, it must be added, as the dominating care) which he so sorely needed.

Lang's Fellowship did not end until 1876, but he was granted 'a year of grace in view of his approaching marriage'—which took place at Christ Church, Clifton, on April 17, 1875. The young couple set up house at 1, Marloes Road, Kensington ('walk along the Cromwell Road until you drop—and then turn right', was Lang's direction to Rider Haggard on his first visit), which remained their home for the rest of Lang's life, though in later years they were accustomed to spend part of each winter at St Andrews on account of his health, which suffered from the London fogs.

'I have scribbled in verse and in prose. . . .
    I can gossip with Burton on *skenes*. . . .
And my name is familiar to those
    Who take in the high-class magazines!'

'Oxford, that once seemed a pleasant porch and
entrance into life, may become a dingy ante-room,
where we kick our heels with other weary, waiting
people. At last, if men linger there too late, Oxford
grows a prison. . . . It is well to leave the enchantress
betimes, and to carry away few but kind recollections,' wrote Lang at the end of his first prose book
Oxford: Brief Historical and Descriptive Notes
(1879), written as a companion volume to Stevenson's *Edinburgh*.

It seems inevitable that a man of his restlessness
of mind and intellect should have rebelled against
the strict academicism of mid-Victorian Oxford
('the abhored pedantic Sanhedrin' as Stevenson
called it), but undoubtedly Lang sometimes
regretted his choice:

'Because within a fair forsaken place
The life that might have been is lost to thee.'

However, the break was only with the outward
and visible trappings of Oxford, the security, and
the weight which 'Fellow of Merton College'
would have added to his more serious labours.
Lang had laid the foundations both for his scholarly
works and for the amazing versatility of his writing

as journalist and man of letters during his years at St Andrews and Oxford, and George Saintsbury doubted whether in the seventies any other young don of either Oxford or Cambridge 'possessed knowledge of ancient and modern literature as literature, coupled with power to make use of that knowledge in a literary way, to a greater extent than Lang.'

For his first few years in London, Lang was making his way as a journalist and securing his position among editors so that he might always have a regular source of income at hand. And in this he prospered so well that he was soon writing two or three literary 'leaders' a week for *The Daily News*, and one for *The Sunday Review*, besides miscellaneous contributions to other dailies and weeklies.

Very soon 'we counted the day empty unless an article by Lang appeared', as Bernard Shaw remembered; and the individuality of his writing made it unnecessary for the articles to be signed. 'His leaders in *The Daily News* read like fairy tales written by an erudite Puck', wrote Richard Le Gallienne. 'No other such combination of poet, scholar and journalist has been known in Fleet Street'; and Saintsbury summed up: 'A good deal of its singular power to delight was no doubt due to the fact that the author himself almost invariably took pleasure in his own work. He very soon proved himself so valuable to editors that nobody thought of imposing mere grind upon him; and he very seldom worked against the grain.' It was this spontaneous delight in writing, and the infectious interest in all that he wrote about which led Oscar

Wilde in 1888 to christen Lang 'the divine amateur'—aptly using the word in both its senses.

Lang soon established himself in the literary London of the seventies, for he brought several useful introductions from Oxford, like that to Spencer Baynes who secured him to write on a variety of subjects for the ninth edition of *The Encyclopaedia Britannica*. His friendship with F. W. Longman led to an even closer friendship with Charles Longman who soon began to employ him as literary advisor to his publishing firm. It was probably another Oxford introduction which led him to Frank Hill of *The Daily News*; and soon he himself was in the position of introducing other young literary aspirants, the earliest being George Saintsbury.

The friendship with Robert Louis Stevenson ripened rapidly: from the moment he read the first essays in *The Cornhill* Lang had realized that 'here was a new writer, a writer indeed', and had helped him in placing further articles and by praising Stevenson's work in his capacity as literary critic. It was Stevenson who introduced Lang to a rather shady editor called Glasgow (or Caldwell) Brown who was starting a weekly paper called *London*. Lang added Saintsbury to the staff, and Stevenson brought in W. E. Henley; the mysterious Brown disappeared, and Henley ran the paper for the rest of its year (1878) of life. Sometimes these four produced the whole paper, Lang contributing verses and some articles, Saintsbury and Henley mainly political leaders and criticism, and Stevenson several essays and *The New Arabian*

Nights. Not long afterwards Lang and Stevenson began to collaborate on an adventure story *Where is Rose?* which got little further than an elaborate plot: 'I and another man plan a sensational novel which probably we won't write!' he confided to his brother John in 1882. Meanwhile Stevenson introduced him to Edmund Gosse in 1877, and he introduced himself to Austin Dobson on the plea of like interests in old French verse forms, and the three of them were soon showing each other their experiments in the shaping of ballades and rondeaux.

Lang collected his first harvest of these beautiful, brittle verses in *Ballades in Blue China* in 1880, which he followed by several other collections both grave and gay. The serious poetry belonged mainly to this, the earlier part, of his career, and for a time it seemed that he might achieve his highest fame as a poet. However his most considerable 'bid for the laurels', the narrative poem *Helen of Troy* (1882) did not prove popular in a period that was already surfeited with such greater works of the same kind as *The Earthly Paradise* and *The Idylls of the King*, and thereafter Lang's muse seemed to desert him— or he drove her firmly away, being one of those who are too easily discouraged. 'Has the Muse gone away?' he wrote to Dobson ten years later. '*Mine* has, for good. She never was very much, always rather a humbug. I have no opinion of her.'

Meanwhile the prose translation of the *Odyssey*, which had been started at Merton, was completed in collaboration with S. H. Butcher, who had already been working on a version of his own, and whose exact scholarship was a useful foil to Lang's more literary skill. The result, published in January 1879, was one of Lang's most successful books, and became an undisputed classic in its own right for fifty years, and has never been out of print, though it is only now escaping slowly from a period of neglect; and the same is true of the companion translation of the *Iliad* which appeared in 1883 and in which Lang had the assistance of Walter Leaf and Ernest Myers. Besides being extremely accurate, and close to the Greek, these two versions are still the nearest approach in English to what the Greeks of the Classical period must have found in the original: for it is often forgotten that Homer used a poetic form of diction, which was archaic even in his own day. Such admirable translators into contemporary prose as E. V. Rieu give us simply the best of all adventure stories, but lose all sense of the poetry, the mystery and the heroic distance of the original. Classical scholars teaching Greek in our universities today are turning back more and more to 'Butcher and Lang' and 'Lang, Leaf and Myers' as the closest and best companions to the original. Just as a young reader will get more out of Malory than from any retelling of the Arthurian legends, so, and in precisely the same way, will he win nearest to the ancient epics in those versions of which Lang was the guiding spirit.

With his translations Lang opened the magic door to the great literature of the past, a particularly important legacy now that a knowledge of Greek is the exception rather than the rule, even among students of literature. To the study of English literature as an academic subject Lang was strongly opposed: 'What is learned of literature, at Oxford, is learned from reading the best literature, that of Greece and Rome, and from reading for human pleasure', he wrote in 1901, 'there *is* no other way. Schools of literature, examinations and all, ought to be abolished.'

None the less Lang can serve as one of the best guides to English as to Greek literature. He was himself an accomplished critic, a form of writing he distinguished sharply from reviewing. 'Writing about contemporary books is the merest journalism. It is pleasant to praise what one thinks good, and to our deeply fallen nature it is not always unpleasant to blame what one thinks bad; but to be literature, writing about books ought to deal with classics— Homer, Molière, Shakespeare, Fielding, and so on.'

Although he wrote many reviews of contemporary authors, Lang as a rule only collected into books his 'reasoned and considered writing on the tried masterpieces of the world', seldom his 'ingenious and entertaining writing about new books'. This brought upon him the denunciation of Hardy and James and George Moore who expected their works to be considered as Literature and subjected to the newly formed 'canons of criticism' rather than to Lang's usual criterion with contemporary novels, whether or not he enjoyed them.

This idiosyncracy about 'modern fiction' became rather extreme in Lang's later years and it is from the seventies and eighties that his best critical work comes. Nearly all that he collected was written then, even if only published later in book form. Such volumes as *Letters to Dead Authors* (1886), *Letters on Literature* (1889), *Old Friends* (1890), *Essays in Little* (1891), and *Adventures Among Books* (1905) are still full of charm and wisdom, introductions or reminders which bring the good things of literature before one with a persuasive enjoyment that is a welcome and perhaps a salutory change from the over-seriousness of the modern 'Science of Criticism'.

These books contain appreciative studies of Stevenson, Kipling and Bridges, all young authors whom Lang was among the first to recognize and welcome as potentially among the great. But for his other discoveries among rather lesser authors such as Rider Haggard, Conan Doyle, Stanley Weyman, and their followers, as for his appreciation of many other contemporaries from 'F. Anstey' to the earlier Henry James, we have to turn to the periodicals of the period, notably to *Longman's Magazine* in which from 1886 to 1905 he wrote monthly his most famous literary *causerie* 'At the Sign of the Ship'—from which, though urged, he refused to make a selection in book form.

Another of his preoccupations during his first ten years in London was in book-collecting, and he wrote numerous articles on the history and practice of this pleasant hobby in *The Saturday Review* and elsewhere, drawing on these for his two classics of 'Bibliomania', *The Library* (1881) and *Books and Bookmen* (1886).

We find him following this pursuit in the early recollections of Ernest Rhys who wrote about

1880 that 'one winter afternoon I did spy that prince of book-hunters, Andrew Lang, whose dark gipsy face looked out of a fur-lined overcoat with a keen gleam of his black eyes'—in the depths of a bookshop.

We can catch a glimpse or two of Lang in the eighties from the reminiscences of his contemporaries: but we have no real picture of a dinner at 1 Marloes Road, where the guests might range from Stevenson and Mrs Molesworth at one end of the decade to Haggard and Kipling at the other. How tantalizing, too, that we cannot 'look in' at luncheon at the Savile Club—perhaps as Kipling remembered it in 1889:

'One heard very good talk at the Savile,' he wrote. 'There was Gosse, of course, sensitive as a cat to all atmospheres, but utterly fearless when it came to questions of good workmanship; Hardy's grave and bitter humour; Andrew Lang, as detached to all appearance as a cloud but—one learned to know—never kinder in your behalf than when he seemed least concerned with you; Rider Haggard, to whom I took at once, he being of the stamp adored by children and trusted by men at sight. . . .'

And yet—how much more we should like to know. Haggard himself, though he included many of Lang's letters in his autobiography, says little that gives a picture of the man 'in his habit as he lived'—though he was by far the closest friend of Lang's middle life: 'You have been more to me of what the dead friends of my youth were than any other man',

37

Lang wrote; and Haggard summed up on the day after Lang's death: 'And so to Andrew Lang, among men my best friend perhaps, and the one with whom I was most entirely in tune, farewell a while.' Earlier he had written: 'of the friend I know not what to say, save that I reckon it one of the privileges of my life to be able to call him by that much-misused name; the tenderest, the purest and highest-minded of human creatures, one from whom true goodness and nobility of soul radiate in every common word and act, though often half-hidden in a jest, the most perfect of gentlemen—such as Andrew Lang.'

Haggard added that 'a certain obtrusive honesty which will out, and an indifferent off-handedness of manner, has prevented him from becoming generally popular,' and unfortunately many of those who have written of him knew Lang only as a casual acquaintance, as, for example, Max Beerbohm—who met him only twice, in old age, and heartily disliked his later critical opinions—who wrote a most brilliant caricature of him (in 1923) which is remembered to Lang's detriment, while those who really knew him respected his wishes, and remained silent about all but his works.

IV. Mythology and Fairy Tales

'The seeds of flowers from isle to isle
  The birds have brought, the winds have
                                blown. . . .
And tales our fathers told erewhile
  Like flowers through all the world are sown.'

With a writer like Andrew Lang, whose life can in
the main consist only of an account of his works,
it is almost impossible to follow his course in a
chronological order. His career, can, perhaps, be
said to fall roughly into two parts: during the
nineties his more literary pursuits slipped further
and further into the background as his interest in
Scottish history awoke, and became more and more
absorbing: this also makes a division in his external
life, since it was from the nineties that he began to
spend more and more time at St Andrews and less
in London. He made a few new friends, the most
notable being A. E. W. Mason, but they were
among men, like Mason, very much younger than
himself, and he mixed less and less in the literary
(or any other) society of London.

Although literary interests may have yielded
second place to historical not long after the point
to which the present sketch has followed him, one
of Lang's chief interests—which remained as
strong throughout his life—has not so far been
touched upon: anthropology. This, in his day,
covered the widest possible field in the study of
early man, and included mythology, folklore, fairy
tales and (to Lang at least) psychic phenomena and

39

superstitions. It is said that his real interest in these studies began with his reading of the medieval 'magicians' at St Andrews: after his intensive study of the literature, history and political experiments of the ancient Greeks during his Balliol years, he turned his attention to anthropology in the widest possible sense, studying while at Merton all the available evidence published by the field anthropologists, as well as chronicles and histories of the past which might contain material on the mythology, folk tales and beliefs of such diverse races as the ancient Greeks, Egyptians and Etruscans, or Mexico and Peru at the time of the Spanish conquests.

At that time Greek, and hence all European and Middle East mythologies, were explained as 'a disease of language' originating in a misunderstanding of the supposed Aryan language and culture from which western civilization was thought to stem. This system, of which Max Müller, the Professor of Philology at Oxford, was the great prophet, was so generally accepted in the eighteen-seventies that it was even taught in schools.

With his wide knowledge of folk tales, Lang put his finger on the weak spot in the philological interpretation of myths: the Black-fellows of Australia and the pre-Cortez Aztecs of Mexico told many of the same folk tales as the Greeks and the Egyptians—but their language had no connection whatsoever with Sanskrit and the original Aryans.

Lang's first attack was made while he was still at Merton in an article 'Mythology and Fairy Tales' (*Fortnightly Review*, May 1873), which holds its important place in the history of anthropology as 'the first full refutation of Max Müller's mythological system based on the Veda, and the first full statement of the anthropological method applied to the comparative study of myths'.

He followed up his attack in 1884 with a volume of essays on various aspects of the subject, *Custom and Myth*, and made his fullest and most enduring statement of the whole case for comparative anthropology in *Myth, Ritual and Religion* (2 volumes) in 1887.

Of course in a subject like this one neither Lang nor anyone else has produced a book which is the 'final word'. None of his works on anthropology and mythology has been in print for many years; only specialized researchers read them now—but no real expert is either uninfluenced by them (even if only at second hand) or denies their importance. Reinach in 1913 declared that by those books Lang had 'conferred a benefit on the world of learning, and was a genius'; in 1951 Professor H. J. Rose in his lecture at St Andrews on *Andrew Lang: His Place in Anthropology* ratified this statement and pointed out the permanent contribution made to the subject by the books mentioned above, and by Lang's life-long devotion to the study of anthropology.

This intensive study of the mythology and folk-lore of all nations is described here because it was the basis of Lang's best-known and most widespread claim to fame and immortality—the collecting and editing of 'The Fairy Book Series'.

Lang's interest in fairy tales, which began in his

41

early childhood, never slackened. 'When I was a little boy I read every fairy tale I could lay my hands on'; and his enjoyment was not dimmed by all his researches into the origins of myths and *märchen*. The Langs had no children of their own, but they had many nephews and nieces and a number of child-friends. These children were inclined to be a little in awe of 'Aunt Nora' (whom one niece described as apt to be like the Queen in *Prince Prigio*), but they all adored 'Uncle Andrew' and he was thoroughly happy and at ease in their company.

He wrote many amusing letters to children, none of which seem to have survived; his favourite cousin, Florence Sellar, remembered the eagerness with which, at about the age of twelve, she would look out for his letters from Merton, and how in the vacation he would write little burlesque plays for her and her brothers and sisters to act—from one, about how the heroes came home from Troy, to find 'Mrs Agamemnon' playing whist with the other ladies of Mycenae, she could still quote a few lines at the age of eighty.

None of his letters to the younger Sellar cousins has survived, nor to his wife's nieces the Grieves of Branxholm Park, Hawick; but a play which he wrote for the Grieves called *The Black Thief* was printed privately for their use in 1882, and a copy has recently been found in America. This is based on the fairy tale of the same name later included in *The Red Fairy Book*, and is a slight but amusing little extravagance, containing many topical allusions, and showing a clever use of bathos and a few good passages of burlesque heroic verse after the manner of Thackeray:

> 'Ladies, or goddesses, or fairies bright,
> We kneel in dumb confusion at your feet;
> The booby trap was never meant for you.'

Two years later Lang dedicated to the Grieve children his first original fairy story, *The Princess Nobody*, which will be dealt with in the next chapter, and in 1887 he made a free translation of the Belgian version by Charles Deulin of *Johnny Nut and the Golden Goose*, which was issued in a sumptuous volume with a delightful dedication to a child-friend, Dorothea Thorpe, afterwards Lady Charnwood.

Two more original fairy stories followed, and it was not until the publication of the first of his fairy-tale collections in 1889 that Lang made use of his wide knowledge of folk literature as a source of entertainment for children. We do not know what inspired him to put together the collection which appeared as *The Blue Fairy Book*: probably he had found his young friends and relations very attracted by the imaginative books he had already produced, and, remembering his own delight in fairy tales as a boy, decided to challenge the prevailing theory that only realistic stories were popular. Joseph Jacobs (friend of Lang and fellow-member of the Folklore Society) must have been at about this time engaged in collecting (to a large extent orally) the folk tales of the British Isles, for his first volume appeared in 1890, but no one until Lang seemed to realize how much there was for children to discover and make their own. Certainly no significant collection of traditional fairy tales had been published during the preceding thirty years. The first half of the century had seen a tremendous growth of interest in folk-lore, with the publication of the first translation of Grimm's *German Popular Stories* in 1823, of Andersen's *Wonderful Stories for Children* in 1846, and Dasent's translation of Asbjornsen and Moe's *Popular Tales from the Norse* in 1859, but in the late 1880's the emphasis was on stories of real life. Making her list of *What Books to Lend and What to Give* in 1887, Charlotte Yonge, out of the 955 publications for children which she mentions, includes only Grimm, Andersen, *The Arabian Nights*, Croker's *Fairy Legends of the South of Ireland*, and Mrs Craik's *The Fairy Book*, besides seven volumes of tales from Greek and Roman mythology, and Annie and Eliza Keary's *Heroes of Asgard*. Of invented fairy stories there are only seven, including *Alice*. Edward Salmon the following year in his *Juvenile Literature as it is* concentrated on stories of adventure, real-life, and child-novels, making the point that there was very little interest in the Fairies in 1888. While writing *The Child and his Book*, the most comprehensive history of children's literature before Harvey Darton, Mrs E. M. Field wrote even more specifically: 'At the present moment the fairy tale seems to have given way entirely in popularity to the child's story of real life, the novel of childhood'; but she added a footnote before her book was published in 1891: 'Since the above was written

44

eighteen months ago, the tide of popularity seems to have set strongly in the direction of the old fairy stories.'

It seems certain, therefore, that both Lang and his publisher, Charles Longman, took a considerable risk with *The Blue Fairy Book*, in spite of the selling power of Lang's name and (partly because of) the many illustrations by H. J. Ford and Jacomb Hood.

Even as late as 1909, when the Fairy Books had become an established series and were selling throughout the world, Lang wrote to his brother John, when asking him to contribute to *The All Sorts of Stories Book*: 'The work is poorly paid because of the expensive illustrations'.

The first edition was of 5,000 copies at six shillings, but to offset the possibility of loss a limited edition of 113 copies, printed on large paper and with a special Introduction by Lang not included in the ordinary edition, was issued for the book-collector at twenty-six shillings.

In this first volume (and Lang of course had no idea that it was to be the first of a long series) is a remarkably astute collection of imaginative stories whose appeal to children is as valid today as when it was first made. It is the choice of someone who obviously himself loved the stories and knew what children would like—he said that, in reading and arranging the contents, he experienced 'perhaps, as much pleasure as the child who reads them or hears them for the first time'. Blue Beard, 'that little tragic and dramatic masterpiece, moves me yet; I still tremble for Puss in Boots when the Ogre turns into a lion; and still one's heart goes with the girl who seeks her lost and enchanted lover, and wins him again in the third night of watching and of tears'. The collection is naturally more varied than in the later volumes and includes some invented stories, as Lang explains in his introduction to the limited edition: 'This collection, made for the pleasure of children and without scientific purpose, includes nursery tales which have a purely literary origin'. It is probably true to say that never before in one book had such a rich assortment been given to children: a version of 'Gulliver in Lilliput' shortened by the poetess May Kendall; of English folk-tales, old favourites like 'Jack the Giantkiller' and 'Dick Whittington'; from France nearly all Perrault's fairytales, including 'Cinderella' and 'The Sleeping Beauty', and others, like 'Beauty and the Beast' and 'The White Cat', by Mme de Ville-neuve and Mme d'Aulnoy; several stories from Grimm, 'The Goose Girl' and 'Hansel and Gretel' among them; four from Dasent's *Norse Tales*, including 'The Princess on the Glass Hill'; Lang's own brilliant retelling from the ancient Greek of the story of Perseus in its original fairy-tale form under the title 'The Terrible Head'; 'The Black Bull of Norroway' and 'Red Etin' from Scottish legend, and three stories from *The Arabian Nights*, 'Aladdin', 'The Forty Thieves', and 'The Story of Prince Ahmed and the Fairy Paribanou'. (In the current edition of *The Blue Fairy Book* these last three stories are omitted, having been appro-priately transferred to Lang's own *Arabian Nights*: 'Gulliver in Lilliput' is also omitted.)

46

In presenting these stories Lang had not only to combat (among adults, who buy the books, rather than the children who read them!) the idea that children were no longer interested in fairy tales, but also in an age when 'the crocodile of Realism' seemed to be winning the battle against 'the catawampus of Romance', against critics and educationists who considered the unreality and escapism in fairy tales to be harmful for young readers (even Charlotte Yonge wrote 'Fairy tales should be regarded as treats'), while such stories were beneath serious consideration as literature that could be enjoyed by adults. Lang would have welcomed Professor J. R. R. Tolkien's energetic defence of fairy tales fifty years later in a lecture at St Andrews (in honour of Lang himself), though perhaps not have gone so far in his insistence that children only enjoy fairy tales by chance in the same way as they enjoy certain other types of literature intended for adults. But he would have been in complete agreement with Tolkien's thesis that fairy tales come even nearer to the ultimate realities than most of the professedly realist and 'adult' novels.

For in his Introduction to *The Blue Fairy Book* Lang wrote that 'when the Princess awakens, after her betrothal to the Yellow Dwarf, and hopes it was a dream, and finds on her finger the fatal ring of one red hair, we have a brave touch of horror and of truth. All of us have wakened and struggled with a dim evil memory, and trusted it was a dream, and found, in one form or other, a proof, a shape of that ring of red hair'. And three years later he was even more explicit when reviewing some anaemic and refined attempts at 'modern' fairy tales:

'In the old stories, despite the impossibility of the incidents, the interest is always real and human. The princes and princesses fall in love and marry—nothing could be more human than that. Their lives and loves are crossed by human sorrows. In many the lover and his lady are separated by a magic oblivion: someone has kissed the prince, and he instantly forgets his old love, and can only be recovered by her devotion. This is nearly the central situation of the *Volsunga Saga*, though there it ends tragically, whereas all ends well in a fairy tale. The hero and heroine are persecuted or separated by cruel stepmothers or enchanters; they have wanderings and sorrows to suffer; they have adventures to achieve and difficulties to overcome. they must display courage, loyalty and address, courtesy, gentleness and gratitude. Thus they are living in a real human world, though it wears a mythical face, though there are giants and lions in the way. The old fairy tales which a silly sort of people disparage as too wicked and ferocious for the nursery, are really "full of matter", and unobtrusively teach the true lessons of our way-faring in a world of perplexities and obstructions.'

The Blue Fairy Book was an instant success, far beyond any possible expectation, and Lang followed it with *The Red Fairy Book* which appeared (in an edition of 10,000 copies) in time for Christmas 1890, saying in his introduction 'The best of all were naturally selected for the earlier volume . . .'

and regretting that 'in a second gleaning of the
fields of Fairy Land we cannot expect to find a
second Perrault. But there are good stories enough
left and it is hoped that some in the *Red Fairy Book*
may have the attraction of being less familiar than
many of the old friends'. In it he included 'Jack and
the Beanstalk', 'The Black Thief and the Knight
of the Glen', 'Soria Moria Castle', 'Dapplegrim',
and, among other stories from Grimm, 'The
Twelve Brothers', 'Rapunzel', 'Snowdrop', and
'The Golden Goose', as well as a version of his
own of the *Volsunga Saga* from William Morris's
translation. But it was still clear that Lang had no
idea that this was the start of a long series of books,
and the next year he produced an anthology of
poetry, *The Blue Poetry Book*.

The first two Fairy books were so successful that
in 1892 what Lang described as 'the third, and
probably the last, of the Fairy books of many
colours' appeared, *The Green Fairy Book*. In his
introduction Lang wrote: 'First there was the *Blue
Fairy Book*; then, children, you asked for more, and
we made up the *Red Fairy Book*; and when you
wanted more still, the *Green Fairy Book* was put
together. . . . If we have a book for you next year, it
shall not be a fairy book.' The book which appeared
the next year was *The True Story Book*. But by now
presumably the series was in the minds of the
public so well established that it was already
considered almost an institution. One can imagine
that Lang accepted with delight what had been
thrust upon him, and each year yet another collection appeared—fairy tales of every colour in the

rainbow, stories of Romance, of Animals, of Heroes, and All Sorts of Stories. In the end the series ran into twenty-five annual volumes (1889-1913), though only twelve of these were Fairy Books. Several others, however, such as *The Arabian Nights*, two *Romance* books, and the final *Strange Story Book*, come almost within the category of 'fairy stories'.

The stories came from all over the world. There is scarcely a country from Ancient Egypt to the obscurest tribes of central Australia that is not represented, and some of the stories (notably those from India) appeared here in print for the first time. After a little initial fumbling in the earlier volumes with their plurality of story-tellers, the evenness and quality of the style maintain an amazingly high standard. Lang himself retold hardly any of the tales in the Fairy Books; at first his Sellar cousins and his wife's nieces, besides several young ladies of a literary turn, translated a number of the stories, and after a time the majority of them were the work of Mrs Lang (whose name, in fact, appears as author on some of the later, non-fairy, volumes). How much Lang himself worked on the final revision or how much of his effortless, lucid style crept into each volume we shall never know. (The exceptions would be in the *True Story* books to which such authors as Rider Haggard and S. R. Crockett contributed, and Lang himself supplied several long items.)

'My part has been that of Adam, according to Mark Twain, in the Garden of Eden. Eve worked, Adam superintended,' wrote Lang in *The Lilac Fairy*

Book (1910). 'I find out where the stories are, and advise, and, in short, superintend. *I do not write the stories out of my own head.* The reputation of having written all the fairy books (a European reputation in nurseries and the United States of America) is "the burden of an honour unto which I was not born".'

Nevertheless it is for the Fairy Books that Lang is best remembered, and rightly so. Whoever did most of the actual writing, the volumes of many colours were completely his, and without his knowledge and his love for fairy tales they would never have come into being. His was the genius and what he did was to give to children a tremendous field for exploration. Many have come after him but time itself cannot reduce the debt children and storytellers owe to him. The books remain a continual source of happiness and imaginative enrichment for children once they can read fluently for themselves.

They begat hosts of rivals and imitations: but who now remembers the *Diamond* or *Ruby Fairy Books* and the rest, even with their excellent illustrations by H. R. Millar? Lang himself certainly owed a good deal to the artist who illustrated twenty-four out of the twenty-five volumes of the series (sharing his labours with other artists in four early volumes, and standing aside only in 1909 when Wallis Mills supplied all the pictures for *The Red Book of Heroes*)—Henry Justice Ford (1860-1941) whose illustrations, with their touch of Pre-Raphaelitism to give grace and beauty to his accurate and forthright interpretations, are among the best and most suitable ever accorded to fairy tales.

The books were constantly reprinted until the beginning of the Second World War, when all the publisher's stock, the blocks and originals of the illustrations, were destroyed in the Blitz of 1940. But Lang's reputation was still very much alive in America where new editions of the coloured Fairy Books were being prepared under the guidance of a general editor, Mary Gould Davis, and it is these editions which are currently in print in England. The books were re-set in a larger type-size than that of the original editions and this made it necessary to cut down the length of the volumes by omitting some of the stories. The American editor tried to limit these omissions to 'those stories that have been systematically "skipped" by two generations of children and by the storytellers'. All of the first six were revised in this way and re-illustrated by modern American artists. The contents of the last six were re-arranged to form the new *Orange* and *Olive* and a completely re-constituted and re-titled *Rose Fairy Book*.*

Besides the Fairy Books, Lang edited *The*

---

* Lang himself never altered the contents of any of the 'Fairy Book' volumes, which remained exact reprints of the first editions until 1940. But Longmans issued many smaller volumes as 'prize books' or school books in a variety of sizes and bindings both during Lang's life and up to the destruction of their stock. These ranged from *Cinderella and Other Stories* (1890) 12mo. price one shilling, by way of *The Magic Ring, and Other Stories from the Yellow and Crimson Fairy Books* (1906), Cr. 8vo price two shillings and sixpence, to *Old Friends among the Fairies* (1926), Cr. 4to price five shillings and the paper-bound *Giants and Dwarfs* (1936) price sixpence: I have traced fifty-one such reprints prior to 1940.

Nursery Rhyme Book (1897) for the firm of Warne. This collection of over three hundred rhymes, arranged under such headings as Historical, Tales, Charms and Lullabies, Games, Riddles and Paradoxes, with an introduction by Lang and illustrations by L. Leslie Brooke, is still a useful and popular selection, having been continuously reprinted since its first publication.

Lang also wrote introductions to several children's books: classics such as Lamb's *Tales from Shakespeare* and Stevenson's *A Child's Garden of Verses*, as well as to contemporary stories or collections such as Mrs Langloh Parker's *Australian Legendary Tales*.

As I have said, Lang himself wrote relatively little in the Fairy Book Series, his longest contributions coming in *The True Story Book* (1893), and *The Red True Story Book* (1895), for the second of which he wrote a seventy-page account of 'The Life and Death of Joan the Maid'—his favourite heroine of fact or fiction. In 1906 he wrote a little biography of her for children, *The Story of Joan of Arc* for a series called 'The Children's Heroes' which his brother John was editing: 'I have got on apace with Miss d'Arc', he wrote, 'but, bless you, the public will *snort* at it. They have no use for dead people, a living Bobs is better than a dead Pucelle. . . . The Maid's doings will sound like flat lies to the public, who will think, if they get so far as to think, that I invented them when drunk. I suppose footnotes are barred, but I have feebly tried to instruct the infant mind as to the nature of the evidence.'

In spite of this typically pessimistic forecast, *The Story of Joan of Arc* was extremely popular, and was reprinted more than thirty times in as many years: a pity that it has slipped out of memory, for it is an excellent little book, and by no means too difficult or out of date for the modern child.

Better known, however, is Lang's inspired re-telling of *Tales of Troy and Greece*, which was published in 1907 as a kind of extra volume to the Fairy Book Series, with illustrations by H. J. Ford. Two-thirds of this book are taken up with the Adventures of Odysseus (under which title it was reprinted, without the extra stories, in Dent's 'Children's Illustrated Classics' in 1962); the rest of the original volume covers the same ground as Kingsley's *The Heroes*, telling shortly of Perseus and Theseus, and including *The Story of the Golden Fleece* which Lang retold for the American magazine *St Nicholas* in 1890, and which was reprinted as a little book in the United States in 1903.

Of the main portion, *The Adventures of Odysseus*, Lang wrote to his brother John in December 1906: 'I have done a lot of a Greek and Trojan book for children. The typist is an enthusiastic student of it. I mainly stick to the Greek of Homer and several other authors, but I had to invent a point or two, where the old Greek poems are lost.'

Besides drawing from sources not usually tapped, such as Quintus Smyrnaeus, Tryphiodorus, and the fragments of the Epic Cycle, even Eustathius and Servius, Lang made excellent use of his in-tensive study of the latest discoveries at Mycenae and Knossos, and is the only reteller of the Homeric story to set the siege of Troy in the age to which it really belonged and of which Homer was telling. In his conviction that Homer sang of a real siege which took place near the end of an actual civilization just before the Dorian Invasion and the fall of Mycenae, Lang was well in advance of the scholars of his time; his supposition has only been proved true by the most recent excavations at Mycenae, Pylos and Athens, and by the decipherment of the 'Linear B' script of the Mycenaeans as early Greek by Michael Ventris in 1952.

Lang's book ranks with and supplements Kingsley's *Heroes*, and in fact an anonymous writer in *The Times Literary Supplement*, (21 November 1958) set him above Kingsley and also Hawthorne, maintaining that of all retellers of Greek myth and legend Lang best understood 'how a child's mind worked' and alone has succeeded in capturing the necessary simplicity of style without losing any of 'the old original music'. The writer ends his admirable study of retellings from the Greek by complaining that in even the best modern attempts 'there is nothing left but a mere *story*—flat, two dimensional, briskly and accurately told, entirely lacking in richness and strangeness, purged of horror and poetry, with no associative splendour in the description from which a child's imagination could catch fire. How one longs for Lang's *Tales of Troy and Greece* to be reprinted; in their chosen field they were, and remain, unequalled.'

As the modern reteller mainly in the reviewer's mind, I can agree whole-heartedly in his estimate of the immeasurable superiority of Lang as master of the perfect style and the poet's touch which transfers the magic from the ancient Greek into the modern English with the smallest possible loss on the way. But it is only fair to add that Lang, besides being an author and a scholar of genius, came at the perfect moment to write such a book. He was living at the peak of a golden age of children's literature when children's literary wants were best understood; and also in the last golden twilight of the old poetic tradition, when he could still write in a prose admirably tinged with the archaic mode and diction, without a touch of the self-consciousness which is apt to make any modern attempt seem stilted and artificial. Also he wrote for a more restricted audience of children with a relatively literate background, and in 1907 had nothing to fear from the blue pencil of the modern Editor of Children's Books—understandably anxious to 'tone down' any difficulties of vocabulary, style or *mise-en-scène*, but perhaps banishing in their zeal for simplicity an unnecessarily large amount of the 'associative splendour'.

'All that wonderful story he told to their pleasure, and Euryalus made amends for his rude words at the games, and gave Odysseus a beautiful sword of bronze, with an ivory hilt set with studs of gold. Many other gifts were given to him, and were carried and stored on board the ship which had been made ready, and then Odysseus spoke goodbye to the Queen; saying: "Be happy, oh Queen, till old age and death come to you, as they come to all. Be joyful in your house with your children and your people, and Alcinous the King." Then he departed, and lay down on sheets, and cloaks in the raised deck of the ship, and soundly he slept while the fifty oars divided the waters of the sea, and drove the ship to Ithaca.'

v. Fairnilee and Pantouflia

'There lived a King once, and a Queen,
As few there are, as more have been,'——
Ah, still we love the well-worn phrase,
Still love to tread the ancient ways. . . .

'There was a time when I regarded all *contes*,
except *contes populaires*, as frivolous and vexatious,'
wrote Lang in 1895, pointing out that the folklorist 'is not unnaturally jealous of what, in some
degree, looks like folklore. He apprehends that
purely literary stories may win their way, pruned
of their excrescences, to the fabulous, and may
confuse the speculations of later mythologists.'
However he soon decided that such a view 'is the
fanaticism of pedantry', and that 'literary fairy
tales may legitimately amuse both old and young,
though "it needs Heaven-sent moments for this
skill".'

That writers of literary fairy stories had been
favoured with such moments Lang was always
ready to admit: 'It is a very difficult thing indeed
to write a good fairy story nowadays,' he wrote in
1905, 'and if I know a really good one it is *The Rose
and the Ring*.' He was also an early enthusiast for
the faery-romances of George MacDonald, though
his favourite was *Phantastes*, 'which the abundant
mysticism does not spoil, a book of poetical adventure perhaps too unfamiliar to children.' Of other
contemporary fairy stories 'the delightful, inimitable, irresponsible nonsense of *Alice in Wonderland*
marks it the foremost,' while 'to speak of Andersen

is superfluous, of Andersen so akin in imagination to the primeval fancy, so near the secret of the heart of childhood.'

How much of that secret Lang knew, and how much of it shows in *The Gold of Fairnilee* and *Prince Prigio* has been disputed. Both stories were extremely popular in their own day, and accepted as classics in their own kind: the American critic Brander Matthews, for example, wrote of *Prince Prigio* in 1894 that he 'unhesitatingly proclaimed it the most delightful of modern fairy tales since *The Rose and the Ring*'. And in one form or another they were steadily reprinted until 1943, after which, for a variety of reasons, largely to do with the publisher who owned the copyright, they went completely out of sight for nearly twenty years. The new edition of *Prince Prigio* and its sequel *Prince Ricardo* in Dent's 'Children's Illustrated Classics' in 1961 is too recent for it to be possible to draw any conclusions, and *The Gold of Fairnilee* has not yet found a new publisher. However, such of the younger generation who have read them have greeted them with enthusiasm, and a young student in a recent thesis on Victorian stories of fantasy ranked *The Gold of Fairnilee* and *Prince Prigio* with MacDonald's *The Princess and the Goblin*, Frances Browne's *Granny's Wonderful Chair*, Mrs Molesworth's *Four Winds Farm* and Ruskin's *The King of the Golden River* as 'the very best Victorian fairy tales for children.'

Lang wrote as it were a prelude to his two best stories, *The Princess Nobody: A Tale of Fairyland* (1884), perhaps unique among fairy tales as being written to fit its numerous illustrations.

These were a series in colour by Richard Doyle which Longmans had published in 1869 in a sumptuous volume called *In Fairyland: Pictures from the Elf World*, accompanied by, but not illustrating, some inferior poems by William Allingham. At Charles Longman's suggestion Lang wrote a cunningly contrived story on the traditional lines, making use of all but four of the original thirty-six pictures (of which a few were divided and printed in several small 'cuts' without colours), and explaining the discrepancies in his main character, Prince Comical, by an ingenious series of transformations. 'Nobody can write a *new* fairy tale; you can only mix up and dress up the old, old stories, and put the characters into new dresses,' he wrote in the Preface to the last of the Fairy Books. This may have been all that he did in *The Princess Nobody*, but the result was an 'extra' fairy tale so good that it can stand alone without the pictures which inspired it, or at least gave Lang the pretext for writing it—as may be seen from the volume of *Modern Fairy Stories* published in 1955 in which it was first reprinted.

In *The Gold of Fairnilee* (1888), the first of his longer fairy stories, Lang experimented in a type of which there are few examples: fairy stories using Fairy in its non-literary sense. The Fairies of the Scottish Border, in whom people still believed at the beginning of the nineteenth century, were the sub-human, slightly diabolical, creatures who play a prominent part in such Ballads as 'Childe Rowland', 'Tamlane' and 'Thomas of Ercildoune'.

Lang wrote that 'the genuine fairy people of Kirk's *Secret Commonwealth* (1691), "The Good Folk", "The Folk of Peace", the dwellers in subterranean palaces or in the shadowy realm beyond the stream of slain men's blood, are not human enough to play any part in the genuine old nursery stories of the world. . . . Visitors to Fairyland are really among the dead, they behold men lost or drowned or fallen in battle. The Fairy Queen in Chaucer is the "Fairy Queen Proserpina" of Campion's song. These mysterious beings who borrow Christian knights, who pay a tax to Hell, who steal children and employ mortal nurses, who carry men away from the edge of the flooded ford, have no connection but in name with Madame d'Aulnoy's capricious *Fées*, who are propitiated with gifts of scissors, ribbons, and candy.'

The Border Fairy is obviously difficult to use in a story for children, and few attempts have been made. Mrs Craik's *Alice Learmont* (1852) seems to have been the only full-length work of the kind before Lang's; it was not a great success, can now only be read as a curiosity, and it is very probable that Lang had never read it. Even George Mac-Donald did not manage to capture a convincing picture of this Fairyland, Highlander though he was by birth and upbringing, and the two short stories which he fitted together as *The Carasoyn* in 1871 are among his least successful. The most satisfactory attempt was that made by another Scot, Mrs Molesworth with the short story 'Con and the Little People' included in her first children's book, *Tell Me a Story*, in 1875; she tried towards the end of her career to depict the same empty, soulless fairland of gilded shadows in *The Ruby Ring* (1904), but with small success. Much more successful in recreating a fairy world of actual tradition was one of Lang's youngest discoveries, Walter de la Mare; but his mocking, heartless, but entirely convincing, English fairies are as far removed from the Border variety as the delicious Irish fairies of *The Crock of Gold*.

Lang's success with his difficult medium in *The Gold of Fairnilee* seems to be complete, though its unusualness and the slightness of the plot have not made the book as generally popular as *Prince Prigio*. Of the plot aspect he wrote to Rider Haggard: 'I dare say you *would* have made more of the Scottish treasure, much to Arrowsmith's advantage, but I can't do fiction; it's only a lot of childish reminiscences of old times in a better place than 1 Marloes Road.' But whatever the story may lack in excitement or suspense, is well made up for by the creation of atmosphere, the realization of setting, the feeling both of the period of the adventures and the universality of the basic experience. It is also one of the most perfect examples of Lang's style, the absolute simplicity and lucidity of the language hiding the skill and finish.

The story tells simply of Randal Ker, born just before the Battle of Flodden, whose home is in the old house of Fairnilee which Lang knew and loved so well, and of the little English girl Jean who is brought home unintentionally from a cattle raid, a tiny baby hidden in a bundle of tapestries. They grow up together, and when he is about thirteen Randal goes by himself to the Wishing Well and asks to be taken to Fairy Land. After this he vanishes for seven years, and is only won back by Jean at the end of this time, bringing with him a flask of the magic water which has enabled him to see the emptiness and deception of the Fairy Queen and her world. At Fairnilee a great famine is threatening the very lives of its inhabitants and of the people on Tweedside; but the Magic Water leads to the discovery of the Gold of Fairnilee, the Roman treasure hidden in the Camp o'Rink on the hill above; Randal is able to buy food from England, and the story ends happily with his marriage to Jean.

If the plot is slight in *The Gold of Fairnilee*, Lang made up for it by the clever and intricate construction of *Prince Prigio* which was published six weeks before *The Blue Fairy Book* in 1889. This, the best known of his original fairy stories, has a natural place in the general development of children's literature between *The Rose and the Ring*, his childhood's favourite, and the stories of E. Nesbit whom he was among the first to welcome with enthusiasm. For Lang to set a story in a literary 'Fairy Court' shows how far he had unbent from the days when, as a rigid folklorist, he had praised Mrs Ewing while reviewing her *Jan of the Windmill* in 1875 because she 'never burlesques things old'; he was soon to reach the point when he was commending Thackeray's treatment of the traditional fairy tale because he 'burlesques it with a kindly mockery'.

Lang does not mock in *Prince Prigio*, he takes the full range and implication of 'Fairy Tale' absolutely seriously—as seriously as Prigio takes himself before his conversion—and uses it as if it were historical background. There is delicious exaggeration, but no actual burlesque—except in Prigio's slightly stilted diction. King Grognio knows his Fairy History so well that he argues, when the Firedrake comes to ravage Pantouflia, that 'of course my three sons must go after the brute, the eldest first; and, as usual, it will kill the first two and be beaten by the youngest. It is a little hard on Enrico, poor boy; but *anything* to get rid of that Prigio!' Prigio, however, whose Christening Curse was 'My child, you shall be *too* clever!' and was at that moment 'lying on the sofa doing sums in compound division for fun, said in the politest way: "Thanks to the education your majesty has given me, I have learned that the Firedrake, like the siren, the fairy, and so forth, is a fabulous animal which does not exist. But even granting, for the sake of argument, that there is a Firedrake, your majesty is well aware that there is no kind of use in sending *me*. It is always the eldest son who goes out first and comes to grief on these occasions, and it is always the third son that succeeds. Send Alphonso, and *he* will do the trick at once! . . ." '

In his scepticism, Prigio takes after the Queen, a most determined person, who will believe in nothing magical, even against the evidence (and she is given abundant examples) of her own eyes. Even when he finds and uses the Fairy Christening Gifts, Prigio does not believe—until he falls in love with the Lady Rosalind, when 'something seemed to give a whirr! in his brain, and in one instant *he knew all about it*! He believed in fairies and fairy gifts, and understood that his cap was the Cap of Darkness and his shoes the Seven League Boots, and his purse the Purse of Fortunatus! He had read all about those things in historical books: but now he believed in them.'

Once converted, Prigio naturally knew better than anyone else the best fairytale method by which to deal with the Firedrake, restore his brothers to life, pacify the angry King, and win the Lady Rosalind. He also knew how to defeat the Christening Curse which had made everyone detest him so much, without losing any of his remarkable cleverness.

'The final wish of Prince Prigio was suggested by the invention or erudition of a Lady', wrote Lang in his Preface. This was his little niece Thyra Alleyne, one of the dedicatees and many years later his literary executor; and she told me also that, in spite of the obvious derivation of his hero's name, Uncle Andrew insisted firmly that 'Prigio' rhymes with 'bridge-ee-o'.

The success of *Prince Prigio* was such that Lang followed it with a sequel, *Prince Ricardo* (1893) which is only a little less successful. It tells the adventures of Prigio's son who, unlike his father, was brought up with all the magic gifts at his disposal—with the result that he depended upon them entirely, and would have come to grief when Prigio substituted shams to test him and was then prevented by a wicked fairy from rescuing Ricardo with the aid of the Wishing Cap, had it not been for the Princess Jacqueline who had been well educated in magic and shape-shifting. The book suffers from its episodic nature, and one inharmonious note is struck in the chapter where 'Prince Ricardo crosses the Path of History' and attempts to set the Old Pretender on the English throne. But otherwise the book has moments of beauty and enchantment which even its predecessor could not equal, and most of it holds the interest even though it lacks the brilliant construction of *Prince Prigio*.

In 1906 Lang tried the strange experiment of writing a series of additions to *Prince Prigio* under the title of *Tales of a Fairy Court*, but the basic idea of trying to write a sequel of this kind proved a mistake, and the result is a comparative failure.

It is for *The Gold of Fairnilee* and the original *Prince Prigio* that Lang owes his secure place among the very few who have written books for children which never grow old nor lose their appeal, and which are read with almost equal, though often different, pleasure by those who have left childhood far behind them:

> 'And you once more may voyage through
> The forests that of old we knew,
> The fairy forests deep in dew.'

VI. 'Dear Andrew of the Brindled Hair'

'One gift the fairies gave me: (three
They commonly bestowed of yore)
The love of books, the golden key
That opens the enchanted door.'

'My mind is gay, but my soul is melancholy,' Lang
once said, and to read his poetry and his prose
fiction is to catch here and there a haunting glimpse
of the melancholy soul, the soul of the true poet,
behind the brilliant façade of the gay mind. As he
grew older the deeper inspiration drew further and
further away—and as he grew more and more
melancholy the gay disguise which earned him the
Press-name of 'Merry Andrew' became more and
more necessary.

Just as the poetry gave place to light and ironic
verse, and then dried up almost completely, so the
fiction was drawn less and less from the wells of the
soul and more and more from the sparkling waters
on the surface: *The Gold of Fairnilee* comes from
the deeper source, *Prince Prigio* and *Prince Ricardo*
are the clever constructions of the gay mind.

In his fiction for older readers the same pattern is
roughly visible. His first novel, *The Mark of Cain*
(1886), has a depth which is lacking from *The
Disentanglers* (1902): both these are forgotten now,
except by a few enthusiasts who read them more
frequently than any others of Lang's books. Their
charm lies in their distinctiveness, the unique touch
which can only be described as 'Langishness',
which made George Gordon describe them in his

D.N.B. article on Lang as 'books of note, and such as no one else could have written'.

In the same year as *The Mark of Cain*, Lang collected his short stories of the previous six years in a volume called *In the Wrong Paradise*—once again a peculiarly 'Langish' volume, but revealing something of the melancholy soul as well as the gay mind at its best.

These books have been out of print for years, though they are not difficult to find and well repay the search. But the next work of fiction in which Lang took part, *The World's Desire* (1890) has constantly been reprinted from that day to this. It was written in collaboration with his friend Rider Haggard, and shows both writers at their best—though not always in complete literary harmony.

The story is a sequel to the *Odyssey*, and as fare for young readers, is as exciting as any of Haggard's unaided romances, though it moves more slowly, and has an occasional passage when the action seems to be held up unnecessarily (usually, it must be admitted, by an exuberance of detail from the vast treasure house of Ancient Egypt in which Haggard was at that date revelling a little too freely). Barrie, in an early review, complained of dull patches, but considered the story 'really striking' when regarded as an allegory, and with superb moments of deeply moving tragedy. It is indeed, besides being a gripping adventure story, an allegory of man's constant search after a divine love, after 'the lips that never can be kissed', of the perfect union which is not of this world:

'Who wins his love shall lose her,
   Who loses her shall gain,
For still the spirit woos her,
   A soul without a stain;
And memory still pursues her
   With longings not in vain!'

Still perhaps seeking subconsciously for 'the lips
that never can be kissed', Lang turned from 'the
visible Helen, the bride and the daughter of mystery, the World's Desire', to tell of Joan the Maid
on his own account in *A Monk of Fife* (1896). 'A
monk of Dunfermline, who continued Fordun's
Chronicle, avers that he was with the Maid in her
campaigns and at her martyrdom', wrote Lang.
'Unluckily his manuscript breaks off in the middle
of a sentence. At her trial, Jeanne said she had only
once seen her own portrait, it was in the hands of a
Scottish archer.' The story purports to be the
continuation of the Chronicle, and the Monk who
writes it was, as a young man, called Norman
Leslie, the archer in whose hand Jeanne saw her
portrait.

'The novel is not my trade,' wrote Lang, 'my
romance . . . would turn out bitterly historical.'
This is fair criticism of *A Monk of Fife* which has
some superbly written scenes, and conveys a
wonderful sense of the devotion and almost religious awe inspired by St Joan, but is badly con-
structed, weak in characterization (except for the
Maid herself), and lacking in the suspense necessary to historical romance of this kind.

Much more successful is Lang's only other full-length novel, the Jacobite romance *Parson Kelly* (1900) in which he collaborated with A. E. W. Mason. Though there is little depth of feeling or characterization, it captures brilliantly the artificiality of the period, the outward glitter over the sordid background, and the strange mixture of desperate loyalty and incompetent organization that characterized the Jacobite plots and intrigues.

Besides actually collaborating with two of them, Lang was always ready with help, encouragement and suggestions for any of the younger writers of the period in whose work he was interested, or who seemed to show real promise even in types of literature with which he could not sympathize.

In his capacity as literary adviser to Longmans many manuscripts by unknown writers came his way, and even if not suitable for his own publisher he would whenever possible help to place a likely manuscript elsewhere. This happened in the case of *King Solomon's Mines* which he saw in manuscript before ever he met Rider Haggard. W. E. Henley, who was 'reader' for Cassells, sent Lang the manuscript for an opinion and Lang strongly advised acceptance—and later backed his belief in the new man by reviewing the book in glowing terms. Cassells did not treat Haggard well, and Lang at once secured him for Longmans.

In 1888 the manuscript of a historical novel by a young doctor from Southsea came to him after being refused by numerous publishers, and he accepted it on the spot—writing straight off his appreciation of *Micah Clarke*, and inviting its author, Conan Doyle, to lunch at the Savile. It was the same when Stanley Weyman's first romance *The House of the Wolf*, was sent to him: Longmans published the book, and Lang made a new friend. Other books came his way only after publication, but his praise of *The Prisoner of Zenda* at the Academy Dinner—'It is the type of story that I love'—helped to ensure its success. With Mason too the first meeting came after the publication of *Morrice Buckler* and led to a warm friendship for several years. As a critic Lang was able to assist and encourage innumerable young writers; he welcomed the first poems of Henry Newbolt and Walter de la Mare to places in *Longman's Magazine*, and helped them to bring out their first volumes in book form.

For children's books of his period, Lang seems to have had less chance to show his appreciation in public—largely because such books were seldom in any proper sense reviewed at that time. Early in his journalistic career he wrote short but interesting reviews for *The Academy* of two books by well-established writers: *Jan of the Windmill* and *The Hunting of the Snark*. A book on the borderline between adult and juvenile, *Vice Versa*, was hailed by him at full-length in *The Saturday Review* and *The Daily News* on the day of publication, and Anstey's success was assured in consequence.

Nearer the end of his career Lang was perhaps the earliest critic to acclaim the genius of E. Nesbit when she made her first assault on her true kingdom: 'I am wholly captivated by those perfect little trumps, Mrs Nesbit's characters in *The*

Treasure Seekers', he wrote in his *causerie* in *Longman's Magazine* for December 1899. 'This is a truly novel and original set of adventures, and of the finest tone in the world. Don't be content to read *The Treasure Seekers*, but give it also to children. They will all bless the name of Mrs Nesbit.' Very soon he was writing to her: 'Many thanks for your book and still more for the children in *The Treasure Seekers*, and the other tales. Their chivalry reminds me of the Great Montrose.'

But after 1900 Lang showed less and less interest in contemporary literature of any sort. Though he praised the early social novels of H. G. Wells, wrote enthusiastically of *The House with the Green Shutters* (George Douglas, 1901), and encouraged Maugham, he said nothing about Conrad or Galsworthy and disliked the earlier George Moore and the later Henry James. His journalism became tired and faded—Gilbert Murray described him to me as writing from force of habit, almost as if it had become a disease.

Unfortunately Lang still needed to write his weekly articles in *The Morning Post* and *The Illustrated London News*: 'If Nora died tomorrow, and I were unemployed,' he wrote to his brother John in 1906, 'my finances would be, after all these thirty-five years, where they were when I was twenty-four. I have not made friends of the Mammons of any sort, and am of little use to other anti-Mammonites'. Yet this state was largely due to his extreme and continuing generosity, not only to his own relations but to anyone, particularly in the world of letters, who was in need.

In 1903 Lang might have been made Warden of Merton (though he did not know this until some years afterwards, and never that it was due to F. H. Bradley that he was not elected) which would have been the perfect solution for his remaining years, freeing him from any need of further journalism, and allowing him to give his full time to the studies after which he hankered more and more—Homer and anthropology.

But he returned to London, and when he had prepared *A Short History of Scotland* for schools, began on the last outstanding book he was to write, *A History of English Literature* (1912) which was published two days after his death. Although he described it to his brother as 'that intolerable and grievous labour', undertaken only for money— 'I'd have written as much for nothing about Homer'—it is, nevertheless, alone among such volumes on literature, a work of literature itself. Into it he put his lifetime of study and appreciation, a love of books so wide that he had to read very few for the first time when writing this volume, and of all those mentioned perhaps not five per cent had been read without enjoyment—and most of these were from the Old and Middle English periods.

In summing up Lang's life-work as a man of letters, George Gordon wrote of *The History of English Literature*: 'Nothing so agreeable, so mellow, so humane has been produced in this kind in English. It is such a book as we should all like to have used when we made our first entry on literary history. . . . He was, indeed, both for his reading and his writing, the greatest bookman of our age.'

Out of his last years one clear picture of Lang has been preserved, by his friend Alice King Stewart with whom he used to stay on his way to or from St Andrews.

'Andrew Lang was tall but inclined to stoop, with a rather slight figure. He was very active for his years. In my mind's eye I see him slouching easily along with his hands in his pockets, but I think that this attitude was to get a better view of things as he walked along. He was supposed not to have the use of one eye, and in the other he wore an unmounted monocle, which always seemed to be popping in and out and was only restrained from loss by a black elastic cord. Certainly with his one good eye he saw more than most people with two. His eyes were dark brown, matching his moustache. He had a fine intellectual head, sometimes held rather to one side when looking at objects, partly because of the blind eye. His hair never looked as if it had recently seen a barber, and the brindled locks, which Robert Louis Stevenson described, were white when I knew him. . . .

'His voice was high-pitched, rather thin in quality, and he had a slight burr in pronouncing the letter "R". He had a habit of cutting short his sentences and moving on to an entirely different topic and, as he was also apt to murmur his words into his moustache, one had to be alert in following his talk. . . .

'Every year he and Mrs Lang used to stay with

me, and I always found him a most charming guest, easily entertained and interested in such a wonderful variety of subjects. With strangers he was not always easy to amalgamate, especially as so many were either afraid of him or wondered what were suitable subjects of conversation. . . . This was largely caused, not from rudeness, but from the fact that he was naturally a shy man and highly strung, moreover he did not suffer fools gladly. He was really tender-hearted to the last degree, even to the fish dangling on his hook when fishing.'

To a great extent this very tenderness of heart was Lang's undoing. What had been mere sensitiveness and pity became an almost pathological escapism. His famous attack on *Tess of the D'Urbervilles* was on Hardy's pessimism and the pain the book gave him, rather than on its literary quality, and towards Russian novels his attitude was much the same—though he made haste to add that 'the genius of Tolstoy, Turgenev and Dostoyevsky there is no denying', and that *Crime and Punishment* 'is, to my thinking, simply perfect in its kind; only that kind happens to be too powerful for my constitution.'

Thus in the early years of the present century Lang, finding little in the newer fiction which he could enjoy, forbore to write of it and retired more and more into the Past, unravelling historical mysteries, studying the habits of primitive man and exploring the world of Homer. Mrs Lang described him towards the end of his life as 'one of that order of persons with whom the Past almost wholly shuts out the Present.'

Something like this had been Lang's gift—or the cross that was given him to bear—from the earliest days. In many fields it limited, and at length stifled all but the mechanical side of his literary gifts. But the genius was there, it 'must out', and it found its most enduring expression in those works by which Andrew Lang qualifies for a place in this series of Monographs. His escape into Fairyland was not that of a boy who never grew up, it was of a boy who wished he had never grown up: he was the full adult, as well as the great scholar and the best-read man of his period, who went back—and so could write of what he found there with an authority that is well-nigh unique, and which gives him the high place which he holds and is likely to continue holding.

How much original genius was Lang's may be disputed: no one can doubt that he holds for us the best keys yet fashioned to the world of Homer, to the fullest joys of the library—and to Fairyland.

Andrew Lang died unexpectedly of *angina pectoris* at 11.50 p.m. on July 20, 1912 at Banchory near Aberdeen, and was buried at St Andrews, the 'little city' which he loved so well, within sound of the sea.

In earlier years it had been his wish to lie 'within the sound of Tweed', not far from Fairnilee; for he once wrote 'If I walk, may I walk there'; and in his 'Ballade of his Choice of a Sepulchre':

76

'Here I'd come when weariest!
    Here the breast
Of the Windburg's tufted over
Deep in bracken. . . .
Bring me here, life's tired out guest,
    To the blest
Bed that waits the weary rover. . . .

Friend, or stranger kind, or lover,
Ah, fulfil a last behest,
    Let me rest
Where the wide-winged hawk doth hover.'

The complete list of Andrew Lang's works comes to about 120 separate books (including pamphlets) and over 150 volumes edited or containing prefaces or prose contributions by him, besides several hundred uncollected poems and over five thousand essays, articles, reviews and letters scattered in periodicals and newspapers between 1863 and 1913. Most of the books and a selection of the poems and articles are listed in my *Andrew Lang: A Critical Biography* published by Edmund Ward in 1946: a full-scale Bibliography, compiled a few years ago, remains unpublished.

The following list is restricted firmly to the writings by which Andrew Lang qualifies for a place in these Monographs. Books included which were not strictly written for young readers are those which, by personal experiment, I have found suitable for those of a more literary turn of mind under the age of eighteen.

PART I: BOOKS FOR CHILDREN

A. ORIGINAL STORIES BY ANDREW LANG

The Princess Nobody. 1884. (Longmans) Illustrated by Richard Doyle. Reprinted in *Modern Fairy Stories* (Dent's Children's Illustrated Classics No. 34) in 1955, with illustrations by Ernest Shepard

The Gold of Fairnilee. 1888. [Also Large Paper Edition of 115 copies] (Arrowsmith) Illustrated by T. Scott and E. A. Lemann. Included in *My Own Fairy Book*, 1895. Shortened version in *The World's Best Stories for Children.* 1930. (Nelson)

Prince Prigio. 1889. [Also Large Paper Edition of 116 copies] (Arrowsmith) Illustrated by Gordon Browne. Included in

My Own Fairy Book (1895) and *Chronicles of Pantouflia*
(1932). Reprinted in 1945 (Harrap) with illustrations by
Robert Lawson. Reprinted in 1961 with *Prince Ricardo*
(Dent's Children's Illustrated Classics, No. 50). Illustrated
by D. J. Watkins-Pitchford
Prince Ricardo of Pantouflia. 1893. [Also Large Paper Edition of
120 copies] (Arrowsmith) Illustrated by Gordon Browne.
Included in *My Own Fairy Book*, *Chronicles of Pantouflia*,
and with *Prince Prigio* (see above)
Tales of a Fairy Court. 1906. (Collins) Illustrated by A. A. Dixon

B. STORIES RETOLD BY ANDREW LANG

The Black Thief: A Play. 1882. (Privately printed)
Johnny Nut and the Golden Goose. 1887. From the French of
Charles Deulin. (Longmans) Illustrated by A. M. Lynen
The Story of the Golden Fleece. 1903. (Altemus, U.S.A.) Illustrated
by Mills Thompson
The Story of Joan of Arc. 1906. (Jack) Illustrated by T. Jellicoe
Tales of Troy and Greece. 1907. (Longmans) Illustrated by H. J.
Ford. Re-issued in 1909 in two volumes ('Longmans Class
Books of English Literature') as *Tales of Troy* and *Tales of
the Greek Seas*. Two-thirds of the whole book reprinted as
The Adventures of Odysseus, 1962, (Dent's Children's
Illustrated Classics No. 53). Illustrated by Joan Kiddell-
Monroe

C. STORIES COLLECTED AND EDITED BY ANDREW LANG

I. 'The Fairy Book Series', published by Longmans

The Blue Fairy Book. 1889. [Also Large Paper Edition of 113
copies, with special Introduction by Lang] Illustrated by H.
J. Ford and P. Jacomb Hood. Reprinted in 1949 with illustrations by Ben Kutcher
The Red Fairy Book. 1890. [Also Large Paper Edition of 113 copies,
with special Introduction by Lang] Illustrated by H. J.
Ford and Lancelot Speed. Reprinted in 1950 with illustrations by Marc Simont
The Blue Poetry Book. 1891. [Also Large Paper Edition of 150
copies] Illustrated by H. J. Ford and Lancelot Speed
The Green Fairy Book. 1892. [Also Large Paper Edition of 150
copies] Illustrated by H. J. Ford. Reprinted in 1949 with
illustrations by Dorothy Lake Gregory
The True Story Book. 1893. [Also Large Paper Edition of 150

copies] Illustrated by H. J. Ford, L. Bogle, Lucien Davis, Charles M. Kerr, and Lancelot Speed

The Yellow Fairy Book. 1894. [Also Large Paper Edition of 140 copies] Illustrated by H. J. Ford. Reprinted in 1950 with illustrations by Janice Holland

The Red True Story Book. 1895. Illustrated by H. J. Ford

The Animal Story Book. 1896. Illustrated by H. J. Ford

The Pink Fairy Book. 1897. Illustrated by H. J. Ford

The Arabian Nights Entertainments. 1898. [Also Large Paper Edition of 75 copies] Illustrated by H. J. Ford. Reprinted in 1951 with illustrations by Vera Bock

The Red Book of Animal Stories. 1899. Illustrated by H. J. Ford

The Grey Fairy Book. 1900. Illustrated by H. J. Ford

The Violet Fairy Book. 1901. Illustrated by H. J. Ford. Reprinted in 1951 with illustrations by Dorothy Lake Gregory

The Book of Romance. 1902. Illustrated by H. J. Ford. Portions reprinted in 1905 as *Tales of King Arthur and the Round Table*

The Crimson Fairy Book. 1903. Illustrated by H. J. Ford. Reprinted in 1951 with illustrations by Ben Kutcher

The Brown Fairy Book. 1904. Illustrated by H. J. Ford

The Red Romance Book. 1905. Illustrated by H. J. Ford

The Orange Fairy Book. 1906. Illustrated by H. J. Ford. Reprinted in 1950 with illustrations by Christine Price

The Olive Fairy Book. 1907. Illustrated by H. J. Ford. Reprinted in 1950 with illustrations by Anne Vaughan

The Book of Princes and Princesses. 1908. Illustrated by H. J. Ford

The Red Book of Heroes. 1909. Illustrated by A. Wallis Mills

The Lilac Fairy Book. 1910. Illustrated by H. J. Ford

The All Sorts of Stories Book. 1911. Illustrated by H. J. Ford

The Book of Saints and Heroes. 1912. Illustrated by H. J. Ford

The Strange Story Book. 1913. Illustrated by H. J. Ford

Note: The modern reprints omit a number of stories from each volume, and stories from other volumes are contained in the reprinted *Orange* and *Olive* Fairy Books. An extra volume was published, containing some of the stories not reprinted in the other volumes:

The Rose Fairy Book. 1951. Illustrated by Vera Bock. (Tales from the *Pink*, *Grey*, *Brown*, *Orange* and *Lilac Fairy Books*)

II. Other Books for Children with Introductions by Lang

The Adventures of Ulysses, by Charles Lamb. 1890. (Arnold)

Australian Legendary Tales, by Mrs Langloh Parker. 1897. (Nutt)

Animal Land, by Sybil Corbet. 1897. (Dent)
A Collection of Ballads. 1897. (Chapman and Hall)
The Nursery Rhyme Book. 1897. (Warne) Illustrated by L. Leslie
   Brooke
More Australian Legendary Tales, by Mrs Langloh Parker. 1898.
   (Nutt)
Tales from Shakespeare, by Charles Lamb. 1899. (Freemantle)
   (Reprinted by Constable, 1903)
The Plain Princess, by Irene Maunder. 1905. (Longmans)
A Child's Garden of Verses, by Robert Louis Stevenson. 1907.
   (Longmans Pocket Library)

PART II: BOOKS FOR OLDER READERS

A. STORIES AND ROMANCES
The Mark of Cain. 1886. (Arrowsmith)
In the Wrong Paradise, and Other Stories. 1886. (Kegan Paul)
The World's Desire. [With H. Rider Haggard] 1890. (Longmans)
   Reprinted (Longmans) 1894 with illustrations by Maurice
   Griffenhagen. Reprinted (Macdonald) 1953 with illustrations
   by Geoffrey Whittam
A Monk of Fife. 1896. (Longmans) Illustrated by Selwyn Image
Parson Kelly. [With A. E. W. Mason] 1900. Frontispiece by
   Gordon Browne
The Disentanglers. 1902. (Longmans) Illustrated by H. J. Ford

B. TRANSLATIONS
The Odyssey of Homer. [With S. H. Butcher] 1879. (Macmillan)
Theocritus, Bion, Moschus. 1880. (Macmillan)
The Iliad of Homer. [With W. Leaf and E. Myers] 1883. (Mac-
   millan)
Aucassin and Nicolete. 1887. (Nutt)
Homeric Hymns. 1899. (Allen & Unwin)

C. LITERARY AND CRITICAL WORKS, etc.
The Library. 1881. (Macmillan)
Letters to Dead Authors. 1886. (Longmans)
Books and Bookmen. 1886. (Longmans)
He. [Parody of Haggard's *She*] 1887. (Longmans)
Letters on Literature. 1889. (Longmans)
Lost Leaders. 1889. (Kegan Paul)
How to Fail in Literature. 1890. (Tuer)
Old Friends. 1890. (Longmans)

Essays in Little. 1891. (Henry. Reprinted later by Longmans)
Alfred Tennyson. 1901. (Blackwood)
The Puzzle of Dickens's Last Plot. 1905. (Chapman and Hall)
Adventures Among Books. 1905. (Longmans)
Sir Walter Scott. 1906. (Hodder and Stoughton)
New and Old Letters to Dead Authors. 1906. (Longmans)
History of English Literature. 1912. (Longmans)

———

Poetical Works. 4 volumes. 1923. (Longmans) Edited by Mrs Lang

PART III: SOME WRITINGS ON
FAIRY TALES, etc.

A. INTRODUCTORY ESSAYS BY LANG TO THE FOLLOWING :—

Grimm's Household Tales. 1884. (Bell)
Apuleius: Cupid and Psyche. 1887. (Nutt)
Lamb: Beauty and the Beast. 1887. (Tuer)
Perrault: Popular Tales. 1888. (Oxford)
Cox: Cinderella Variants. 1893. (Nutt)
Kirk: Secret Commonwealth of Elves, Fauns and Fairies. 1893.
   (Nutt)

B. A SELECTION OF LANG'S UNCOLLECTED ARTICLES ON FAIRY TALES, etc.

Scottish Nursery Tales. *St Andrews University Magazine,* April
   1863
Mythology and Fairy Tales. *The Fortnightly Review,* May 1873
Review: 'The Hunting of the Snark'. *The Academy,* 8 April 1876
Review: 'Jan of the Windmill'. *The Academy,* 15 July 1876
Popular Tales in Homer. *The Saturday Review,* 28 July 1877
The Folk-lore of France. *The Folklore Record,* 1878
'Rashin Coatie' and 'Nicht, Nought, Nothing' [Traditional tales
   collected orally by Lang]. *Revue Celtique,* 1878
A Galloway Nursery Tale. *The Academy,* 17 October 1885
Popular Tales. *The Saturday Review,* 25 December 1886
The Story of the Dead Wife. *Murray's Magazine,* April 1887
English and Scotch Fairy Tales. *Folklore* September, 1890
Modern Fairy Tales. *The Illustrated London News,* 3 December
   1892

Literary Fairy Tales. Van Eeden's *Little Johannes*, 1895
Review: 'The Second Jungle Book'. *Cosmopolis*, January 1896
Genius in Children. *North American Review*, January 1897
Fairy Stories. *Literature*: Christmas Supplement, December 1899
Irish Fairies. *The Morning Post*, 15 October 1901
Fairy Godmothers. *The Illustrated London News*, 5 January 1907
Hawthorne's Tales of Old Greece. *The Independent*. (N.Y.), 4 April 1907
The Irish Type of Fairy. *The Morning Post*, 28 June 1907
Where the Fairies Dwell. *The Morning Post*, 1 January 1909
Black Fairies. *The Morning Post*, 19 February 1909
Highland Fairies. *The Morning Post*, 21 January 1910

PART IV: WRITINGS ABOUT ANDREW LANG

A New Friendship's Garland. Poems to Andrew Lang, collected and printed privately by C. M. Falconer, 1899
Andrew Lang: 1844-1912. Pamphlet by P. Hume Brown, 1912
Andrew Lang: Commemorative Articles by R. S. Rait, Gilbert Murray, Solomon Reinach, J. H. Millar. *Quarterly Review*, April 1913
Andrew Lang and St Andrews. A Centenary Anthology, edited by J. B. Salmond (St Andrews University Press), 1944
Andrew Lang: A Critical Biography. By Roger Lancelyn Green (Edmund Ward), 1946
Concerning Andrew Lang. Lang Lectures 1927-37 by G. S. Gordon, A. Shewan, R. R. Marett, R. S. Rait, L. Cazamain, John Buchan, H. J. P. Grierson, J. D. Mackie, Bernard Darwin, A. Blyth Webster (O.U.P.), 1949
[There have been subsequent lectures on Lang, published separately, by Gilbert Murray, Lord Macmillan, J. B. Black, J. B. Salmond, H. J. Rose and W. C. Dickenson. A lecture by J. R. R. Tolkien, delivered in 1940, was re-written at considerable length and included in *Essays Presented to Charles Williams* (O.U.P.), 1947 as 'On Fairy Stories']

There have been many articles on Andrew Lang; among them may be mentioned those by Brander Matthews (*Century Magazine*, January 1894), G. K. Chesterton (*Illustrated London News*, 27 July 1912), Edmund Gosse (*Portraits and Sketches*, 1913), Horace Hutchinson (*Portraits of the Eighties*, 1920), George

Saintsbury (*Quarterly Review*, October 1923; *A Scrapbook*, 1922; *The Eighteen Seventies*, 1929), George Gordon (*D.N.B.* 1927; *The Lives of Authors*, 1950), Max Beerbohm (*Life and Letters*, June 1928), Malcolm Elwin (*The Old Gods Falling*, 1939), Ella Christie and Alice King Stewart (*A Long Look at Life*, 1940), D'Arcy W. Thompson (*Scots Magazine*, May 1944), Roger Lancelyn Green (*English*, July 1944; *Review of English Studies*, July 1944; *Tellers of Tales*, 1946; *A. E. W. Mason*, 1952), and two anonymous articles in *The Times Literary Supplement*—'Coats of Many Colours', 23 November 1951, on the Fairy Books, and 'The 'Heroic Age', 21 November 1958, on Greek legends, with special reference to *Tales of Troy and Greece*